Christmas Movie Bingo
Volume 1

By Nannette Smith

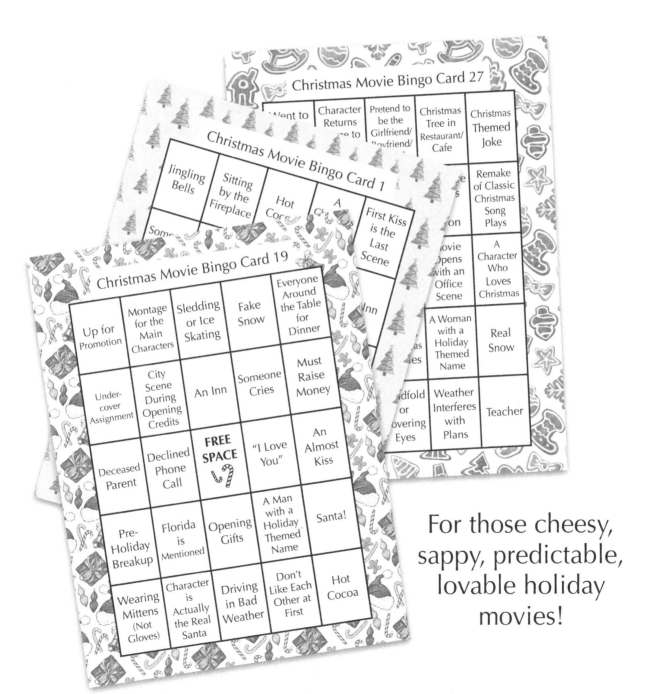

For those cheesy, sappy, predictable, lovable holiday movies!

Christmas Movie Bingo Card 1

Jingling Bells	Sitting by the Fireplace	Hot Cocoa	A Christmas Play or Concert	First Kiss is the Last Scene
Someone is a Scrooge	Christmas Caroling	Wise Parental Advice	Pretend to be the Girlfriend/ Boyfriend/ Fiancé	An Inn
Accidental Fall	Dream Job	**FREE SPACE**	An Apology	Vehicle Breaks Down
City Scene During Opening Credits	Shopping for a Christmas Tree	Wrapping Presents	Sheriff or Doctor is a Main Character	Santa!
Someone is Wearing Plaid	Remake of Classic Christmas Song Plays	Decorating a Christmas Tree	Job Offer	Sledding or Ice Skating

Christmas Movie Bingo Card 2

Holds Mug with Two Hands	Small Town Business is in Trouble	Fireplace Scene	Main Character Lost a Parent	Amnesia
An Injury	Wise Words from a Parent	Match-maker Friend/ Family Member	Single Parent	New York is Mentioned
Someone is Stranded	Santa Suit	**FREE SPACE**	Baking Christmas Cookies	Special Family Tradition
Childhood Home/ Lodge/ Getaway	Working on Christmas	Christmas Tree Farm	Sleigh Ride	Love Triangle
Someone Cries	An Almost Kiss	Kiss Under the Mistletoe	Teacher	A Gazebo

Christmas Movie Bingo Card 3

A Character Who Loves Christmas	Town Event in Jeopardy	"I Love You"	Can't Stay in Town for Long	Under-cover Assignment
Small Diner or Cafe	Character Returns Home to Small Town	Singing a Christmas Carol While Working	An Airport Scene	Montage for the Main Characters
Special Christmas Ornament	Green Grass	**FREE SPACE**	Someone is a Work-a-holic	Leading Man Drives Pickup Truck
A Christmas Party	Wearing a Santa Hat with Normal Clothes	Remake of Classic Christmas Song Plays	Character is Actually the Real Santa	Opening Gifts
Nativity Scene	A Contest	Reindeer	Pre-Holiday Breakup	Sticker Over the Laptop Logo

Christmas Movie Bingo Card 4

Secondary Love Story with Secondary Characters	Niece or Nephew	Christmas Shopping	Jealousy	A Family Heirloom
Must Raise Money	Someone says "Christmas Miracle" or "Christmas Magic"	It's Snowing!	Everyone Around the Table for Dinner	Inherits a Building
Looking at Old Pictures	Doing Something for Charity	**FREE SPACE**	Dancing	Dream Job
Video Chat	Road Trip	Declined Phone Call	Has Child From Previous Marriage	Weather Interferes with Plans
Aerial Shot of a Small Town	Takes a Selfie Photo	Sledding or Ice Skating	Christmas Pajamas	Real Snow

Christmas Movie Bingo Card 5

Cancelled Flight	Making a Snowman	Riding in a Taxi	A Gift of Jewelry	Someone Wears an Apron
Christmas Eve Deadline	Wearing Mittens (Not Gloves)	Hot Cocoa	Went to High School Together	Someone Gets Fired
Christmas Caroling	Looking at Old Pictures	**FREE SPACE**	Baking Christmas Cookies	An Apology
An Almost Kiss	Love Triangle	Bump into Each Other	Fireplace Scene	Product Placement for Advertisement
Roads are Closed	Shirtless Man	Character Returns Home to Small Town	Journalist	A Barn

Christmas Movie Bingo Card 6

Thanks-giving Dinner	Small Town Business is in Trouble	Mismatch Christmas Tree Ornaments	Church Service Scene	Wears a Fancy Dress
Hot Cocoa	It's Snowing!	Someone is a Scrooge	Red Winter Coat	Someone is Lying
Montage for the Main Characters	Sticker Over the Laptop Logo	**FREE SPACE** 	A Kiss with a Foot Pop	Christmas Themed Joke
Obnox-ious Girlfriend or Boyfriend	Character is Royalty	Opening Gifts	Terrible Boss	Sitting by the Fireplace
Small Diner or Cafe	Reindeer	Someone Cries	City Scene During Opening Credits	Blindfold or Covering Eyes

Christmas Movie Bingo Card 7

A Nutcracker Decoration	Decorating a Christmas Tree	Someone Cries	Baking Christmas Cookies	Running Late
Child Wise Beyond Their Years	Coffee Shop	Looking at Old Pictures	Montage for the Main Characters	Dream Job
Character Makes a U-Turn, Literally or Figuratively	Quits Their Job	**FREE SPACE**	"I Love You"	Snowball Fight
Accidental Fall	Red Winter Coat	An Apology	Jealousy	Everyone Around the Table for Dinner
Santa!	Wrapping Presents	Wearing Mittens (Not Gloves)	Main Character Lost a Parent	Single Parent

Christmas Movie Bingo Card 8

An Inn	Driving in Bad Weather	Former Girlfriend/ Boyfriend	Movie Opens with an Office Scene	Putting up Lights Outside
Christmas Shopping	Baking Christmas Cookies	Florida is Mentioned	Must Raise Money	A Christmas Play or Concert
Concerned Family Member	Niece or Nephew	FREE SPACE	Don't Like Each Other at First	Declined Phone Call
Ginger- bread Houses	Movie Opens with a Baking Scene	Lose the Contest/ Competition	Childhood Home/ Lodge/ Getaway	Reindeer
Shopping for a Christmas Tree	Snow Globe	Sheriff or Doctor is a Main Character	Love Triangle	It's Snowing!

Christmas Movie Bingo Card B

Christmas Movie Bingo Card 9

Aerial Shot of Town Decorated for Christmas	A Character Doesn't Like Christmas	Everyone Around the Table for Dinner	Decorating a Christmas Tree	Real Snow
Hand-written Note or Letter	A Gazebo	Christmas Tree in Restaurant/ Cafe	Up for Promotion	Sleigh Ride
First Kiss is the Last Scene	Christmas Pajamas	**FREE SPACE**	Bad Baker/ Cook	Don't Like Each Other at First
Sledding or Ice Skating	Looking at Old Pictures	Santa Suit	Aerial Shot of a Small Town	Characters go to a Fancy Restaurant
Fake Snow	Went to High School Together	An Almost Kiss	Someone is Wearing Plaid	Nativity Scene

Christmas Movie Bingo Card 10

Hot Cocoa	Christmas Tree Falls Over	Match-maker Friend/ Family Member	A Man with a Holiday Themed Name	Ginger-bread Houses
Aerial Shot of Town Decorated for Christmas	Live Christmas Music	"Open" Sign at a Business	Doing Something for Charity	Santa Gives Sage Advice
Character is Actually the Real Santa	Someone Wears an Apron	FREE SPACE	A Scene When It's Not Winter	Secondary Love Story with Secondary Characters
"I Love You"	Product Placement for Advertise-ment	Sitting by the Fireplace	Town Event in Jeopardy	Holiday Party
Amazing Baker/ Cook	Town has a Holiday Themed Name	It's Snowing!	Red Winter Coat	Dream Job

Christmas Movie Bingo Card 11

Special Family Tradition	Main Character has an Office Job	Love Triangle	Fake Snow	Small Town Business is in Trouble
Baking Christmas Cookies	Sledding or Ice Skating	An Apology	Snowed In	A Nutcracker Decoration
Can't Stay in Town for Long	Jealousy	**FREE SPACE**	Deceased Parent	Someone Wears an Apron
Christmas Shopping	Character Returns Home to Small Town	Looking at Old Pictures	Decorating a Christmas Tree	Riding in a Taxi
Declined Phone Call	Wise Parental Advice	Someone Cries	Weather Interferes with Plans	Character Makes a U-Turn, Literally or Figuratively

Christmas Movie Bingo Card 12

Amnesia	Santa Suit	Pre-Holiday Breakup	Wearing Mittens (Not Gloves)	Someone is Stranded
Someone Winks	Driving in Bad Weather	Don't Like Each Other at First	An Inn	Someone Wears an Apron
Tree Lighting	Ugly Christmas Sweater	**FREE SPACE**	Video Chat	Green Grass
Singing a Christmas Carol While Working	Product Placement for Advertise-ment	A Contest	Kiss Under the Mistletoe	New York is Mentioned
Making a Family Recipe	Someone Makes a Wish	A Nutcracker Decoration	Love Triangle	Win the Contest/ Competition

Christmas Movie Bingo Card 13

Red Winter Coat	Leading Man Drives Pickup Truck	A Wedding Scene	Looking at Old Pictures	Christmas Caroling
Christmas Shopping	Someone is a Work-a-holic	Small Diner or Cafe	A Dog	Accidental Fall
Roads are Closed	Montage for the Main Characters	**FREE SPACE** ❄	It's Snowing!	Holds Mug with Two Hands
Someone is a Scrooge	Baking Christmas Cookies	Fireplace Scene	Someone Commits a Crime	Niece or Nephew
Inherits a Building	Hot Cocoa	Must Raise Money	Town Event in Jeopardy	Remake of Classic Christmas Song Plays

Christmas Movie Bingo Card 14

Amazing Baker/ Cook	Mis-under-standing Keeps Them Apart	Takes a Selfie Photo	An Injury	A Character Who Loves Christmas
Son/ Daughter Wants Their Mom/Dad to Get Married	Character Returns Home to Small Town	Dancing	Florida is Mentioned	Wrapping Presents
Love Triangle	Making a Family Recipe	FREE SPACE 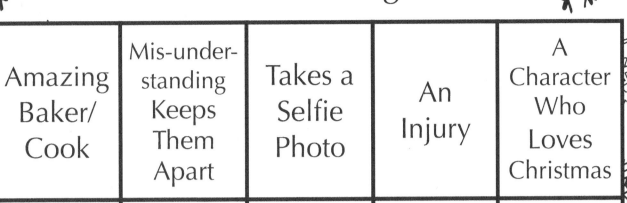	Decorating a Christmas Tree	Christmas Eve Deadline
Reindeer	Declined Phone Call	Looking at Old Pictures	Someone is Lying	Baking Christmas Cookies
Lose the Contest/ Competition	A Woman with a Holiday Themed Name	Small Diner or Cafe	Live Christmas Music	A Contest

Christmas Movie Bingo Card 15

Christmas Tree in Restaurant/ Cafe	Christmas Caroling	An Apology	Sledding or Ice Skating	Must Raise Money
Outsider Puts on Tree Topper	Thanks-giving Dinner	Ginger-bread Houses	Baking Christmas Cookies	Someone Wears an Apron
Jealousy	"I Love You"	**FREE SPACE**	Hand-written Note or Letter	Dream Job
An Old Flame Reappears	Don't Like Each Other at First	An Almost Kiss	Cancelled Flight	Man in a Flannel Shirt
Quits Their Job	Single Parent	Someone Gets Fired	Character is Royalty	Christmas Tree Falls Over

Christmas Movie Bingo Card 16

Blindfold or Covering Eyes	Someone is Wearing Plaid	Looking at Old Pictures	Went to High School Together	Christmas Pajamas
Real Snow	Sitting by the Fireplace	Wearing Mittens (Not Gloves)	Strained Parent/ Child Relation- ship	Shopping for a Christmas Tree
Child Wise Beyond Their Years	Former Girlfriend/ Boyfriend	**FREE SPACE**	Jingling Bells	Accidental Fall
Match- maker Friend/ Family Member	Nativity Scene	Mismatch Christmas Tree Ornaments	Concerned Family Member	It's Snowing!
Love Triangle	Aerial Shot of a Small Town	An Apology	Has Child From Previous Marriage	Doing Something for Charity

Christmas Movie Bingo Card 17

Small Diner or Cafe	A Christmas Play or Concert	A Nutcracker Decoration	Road Trip	Someone has a Secret Identity
Weather Interferes with Plans	Main Character Lost a Parent	Sticker Over the Laptop Logo	Someone is a Scrooge	"Open" Sign at a Business
Santa Suit	Christmas Tree Farm	FREE SPACE	Everyone Around the Table for Dinner	Small Town Business is in Trouble
Opening Gifts	Christmas Themed Joke	Someone is Stranded	Obnoxious Girlfriend or Boyfriend	Christmas Shopping
"I Love You"	Red Winter Coat	Characters go to a Fancy Restaurant	Wearing a Santa Hat with Normal Clothes	Wise Words from a Parent

Christmas Movie Bingo Card 18

Strained Parent/ Child Relation- ship	Stuck in Small Town for Christmas	An Airport Scene	Bump into Each Other	Hot Cocoa
Job Offer	Snow Globe	It's Snowing!	Montage for the Main Characters	A Kiss with a Foot Pop
Sledding or Ice Skating	Aerial Shot of Town Decorated for Christmas	**FREE SPACE**	Making a Family Recipe	Ginger- bread Houses
A Family Heirloom	Niece or Nephew	Amazing Baker/ Cook	Character Returns Home to Small Town	Christmas Tree in Restaurant/ Cafe
A Contest	Baking Christmas Cookies	Putting up Lights Outside	Town Event in Jeopardy	Snowed In

Christmas Movie Bingo Card 19

Up for Promotion	Montage for the Main Characters	Sledding or Ice Skating	Fake Snow	Everyone Around the Table for Dinner
Under-cover Assignment	City Scene During Opening Credits	An Inn	Someone Cries	Must Raise Money
Deceased Parent	Declined Phone Call	FREE SPACE	"I Love You"	An Almost Kiss
Pre-Holiday Breakup	Florida is Mentioned	Opening Gifts	A Man with a Holiday Themed Name	Santa!
Wearing Mittens (Not Gloves)	Character is Actually the Real Santa	Driving in Bad Weather	Don't Like Each Other at First	Hot Cocoa

Christmas Movie Bingo Card 20

Running Late	A Character Who Loves Christmas	A Nutcracker Decoration	Making a Family Recipe	Baking Christmas Cookies
Kiss Under the Mistletoe	Went to High School Together	Childhood Home/ Lodge/ Getaway	A Scene When It's Not Winter	Santa Suit
Everyone Around the Table for Dinner	Terrible Boss	**FREE SPACE**	Live Christmas Music	Main Character Lost a Parent
Someone Wears an Apron	A Christmas Party	Sitting by the Fireplace	Christmas Tree Falls Over	Someone Winks
Dream Job	Decorating a Christmas Tree	Niece or Nephew	A Gazebo	Someone says "Christmas Miracle" or "Christmas Magic"

Christmas Movie Bingo Card 20...

Christmas Movie Bingo Card 21

Sleigh Ride	Wrapping Presents	Baking Christmas Cookies	Jealousy	Aerial Shot of Town Decorated for Christmas
Christmas Tree in Restaurant/ Cafe	Remake of Classic Christmas Song Plays	Christmas Pajamas	A Gift of Jewelry	A Dog
Someone Wears an Apron	Win the Contest/ Competition	FREE SPACE	Roads are Closed	Must Raise Money
A Woman with a Holiday Themed Name	Accidental Fall	Love Triangle	Single Parent	Sledding or Ice Skating
"I Love You"	Christmas Shopping	Snowball Fight	Holiday Party	An Apology

Christmas Movie Bingo Card 22

Vehicle Breaks Down	Main Character has an Office Job	Coffee Shop	Surprise Decorating for Christmas	Wearing Mittens (Not Gloves)
Holds Mug with Two Hands	Someone is Stranded	Leading Man Drives Pickup Truck	Can't Stay in Town for Long	Wearing a Santa Hat with Normal Clothes
Character Makes a U-Turn, Literally or Figuratively	Lose the Contest/ Competition	**FREE SPACE**	Baking Christmas Cookies	Went to High School Together
A Character Doesn't Like Christmas	New York is Mentioned	Santa Suit	Looking at Old Pictures	Dream Job
Red Winter Coat	Character Returns Home to Small Town	Christmas Shopping	Snowed In	Declined Phone Call

Christmas Movie Bingo Card 23

Gingerbread Houses	Wears a Fancy Dress	An Almost Kiss	Inherits a Building	Amnesia
Don't Like Each Other at First	Doing Something for Charity	Town Event in Jeopardy	Ugly Christmas Sweater	Someone is a Work-a-holic
Making a Family Recipe	Someone is Wearing Plaid	**FREE SPACE**	Shirtless Man	Video Chat
Main Character Lost a Parent	Someone is a Scrooge	Wearing Mittens (Not Gloves)	City Scene During Opening Credits	Has Child From Previous Marriage
Snow Globe	Aerial Shot of a Small Town	Riding in a Taxi	Red Winter Coat	Someone Commits a Crime

Christmas Movie Bingo Card 24

Green Grass	An Apology	Hot Cocoa	Bad Baker/ Cook	Baking Christmas Cookies
Nativity Scene	An Almost Kiss	A Contest	Someone Cries	Former Girlfriend/ Boyfriend
Movie Opens with a Baking Scene	Dancing	FREE SPACE	Baking Christmas Cookies	Santa Suit
Small Town Business is in Trouble	Opening Gifts	Montage for the Main Characters	Shopping for a Christmas Tree	Everyone Around the Table for Dinner
Fireplace Scene	Doing Something for Charity	A Barn	Sticker Over the Laptop Logo	Child Wise Beyond Their Years

Christmas Movie Bingo

Christmas Movie Bingo Card 25

Aerial Shot of Town Decorated for Christmas	Sheriff or Doctor is a Main Character	Amazing Baker/ Cook	A Christmas Party	Mis-under-standing Keeps Them Apart
Decorating a Christmas Tree	Love Triangle	"I Love You"	Florida is Mentioned	Driving in Bad Weather
Concerned Family Member	Singing a Christmas Carol While Working	**FREE SPACE**	Thanks-giving Dinner	Match-maker Friend/ Family Member
Cancelled Flight	Looking at Old Pictures	Character is Actually the Real Santa	An Inn	An Old Flame Reappears
"Open" Sign at a Business	Sitting by the Fireplace	Small Diner or Cafe	It's Snowing!	Military Personnel

Christmas Movie Bingo Card 26

Bump into Each Other	Putting up Lights Outside	An Inn	Jealousy	Christmas Tree Falls Over
Hot Cocoa	Town has a Holiday Themed Name	Hanukkah is Mentioned or Decor Seen	A Wedding Scene	First Kiss is the Last Scene
Declined Phone Call	Character is Royalty	**FREE SPACE**	Main Character has an Office Job	Stuck in Small Town for Christmas
Church Service Scene	Must Raise Money	Live Christmas Music	Someone is a Scrooge	Kiss Under the Mistletoe
Baking Christmas Cookies	Accidental Fall	Takes a Selfie Photo	Someone Wears an Apron	A Christmas Play or Concert

Christmas Movie Bingo Card 27

Went to High School Together	Character Returns Home to Small Town	Pretend to be the Girlfriend/ Boyfriend/ Fiancé	Christmas Tree in Restaurant/ Cafe	Christmas Themed Joke
Wearing Mittens (Not Gloves)	Snowed In	Amazing Baker/ Cook	Someone Wears an Apron	Remake of Classic Christmas Song Plays
Secondary Love Story with Secondary Characters	An Injury	**FREE SPACE**	Movie Opens with an Office Scene	A Character Who Loves Christmas
Someone Cries	Don't Like Each Other at First	Baking Christmas Cookies	A Woman with a Holiday Themed Name	Real Snow
Opening Gifts	Reindeer	Blindfold or Covering Eyes	Weather Interferes with Plans	Teacher

Christmas Movie Bingo Card

Christmas Movie Bingo Card 28

An Almost Kiss	Special Christmas Ornament	An Apology	A Gazebo	Lose the Contest/ Competition
Someone is a Work-a-holic	Small Diner or Cafe	Son/ Daughter Wants Their Mom/Dad to Get Married	An Almost Kiss	Montage for the Main Characters
Road Trip	Ginger-bread Houses	FREE SPACE 	Wears a Fancy Dress	Christmas Eve Deadline
Obnox-ious Girlfriend or Boyfriend	Deceased Parent	Sledding or Ice Skating	Santa Suit	Wrapping Presents
Hot Cocoa	Someone is a Scrooge	Driving in Bad Weather	Dream Job	Decorating a Christmas Tree

Christmas Movie Bingo Card 29

Montage for the Main Characters	Opening Gifts	Aerial Shot of Town Decorated for Christmas	Up for Promotion	Wears a Fancy Dress
Someone Cries	"I Love You"	Someone is a Scrooge	Christmas Shopping	Dream Job
Christmas Pajamas	Man in a Flannel Shirt	FREE SPACE	Sitting by the Fireplace	A Family Heirloom
Love Triangle	Fake Snow	Sledding or Ice Skating	Santa Suit	Quits Their Job
Everyone Around the Table for Dinner	A Contest	An Airport Scene	Hot Cocoa	Someone is Lying

Christmas Movie Bingo Card 30

A Scene When It's Not Winter	Tree Lighting	Journalist	Holds Mug with Two Hands	Making a Snowman
Wise Words from a Parent	Childhood Home/ Lodge/ Getaway	Nativity Scene	Red Winter Coat	Baking Christmas Cookies
Snowball Fight	Amazing Baker/ Cook	**FREE SPACE** 	Welcome to Town Sign	Declined Phone Call
Decorating a Christmas Tree	Christmas Caroling	A Nutcracker Decoration	An Airport Scene	Characters go to a Fancy Restaurant
Video Chat	Green Grass	Hot Cocoa	Florida is Mentioned	Working on Christmas

Christmas Movie Bingo Card 31

Wearing a Santa Hat with Normal Clothes	Kiss Under the Mistletoe	Making a Family Recipe	Special Family Tradition	Small Diner or Cafe
New York is Mentioned	Must Raise Money	Single Parent	Win the Contest/ Competition	Accidental Fall
Live Christmas Music	A Nutcracker Decoration	FREE SPACE	Aerial Shot of Town Decorated for Christmas	Former Girlfriend/ Boyfriend
Looking at Old Pictures	Small Town Business is in Trouble	Christmas Shopping	Sledding or Ice Skating	Opening Gifts
Baking Christmas Cookies	Fireplace Scene	Someone is a Scrooge	A Proposal	Wise Parental Advice

			FREE SPACE	

Christmas Movie Bingo Card 32

Ugly Christmas Sweater	Town Event in Jeopardy	Decorating a Christmas Tree	It's Snowing!	Someone Wears an Apron
Someone has a Secret Identity	Looking at Old Pictures	Someone is Stranded	Aerial Shot of a Small Town	"I Love You"
Town Event in Jeopardy	An Inn	**FREE SPACE**	Santa Suit	Character is Actually the Real Santa
Shopping for a Christmas Tree	Character Makes a U-Turn, Literally or Figuratively	Someone Makes a Wish	Accidental Fall	Concerned Family Member
City Scene During Opening Credits	Christmas Tree Falls Over	Weather Interferes with Plans	Don't Like Each Other at First	Jingling Bells

Christmas Movie Bingo Card 33

It's Snowing!	Snow Globe	Santa Gives Sage Advice	Character Returns Home to Small Town	Someone is a Scrooge
Someone Winks	A Character Who Loves Christmas	Holds Mug with Two Hands	Baking Christmas Cookies	Sitting by the Fireplace
A Dog	Dream Job	**FREE SPACE**	Don't Like Each Other at First	Someone is Wearing Plaid
Someone Cries	Someone is a Work-a-holic	Niece or Nephew	Went to High School Together	Inherits a Building
Wearing Mittens (Not Gloves)	Jealousy	A Kiss with a Foot Pop	Thanks-giving Dinner	An Apology

Christmas Movie Bingo Card 34

Holiday Party	Riding in a Taxi	Decorating a Christmas Tree	Dancing	An Apology
Opening Gifts	Concerned Family Member	Everyone Around the Table for Dinner	Love Triangle	Child Wise Beyond Their Years
Remake of Classic Christmas Song Plays	Christmas Shopping	FREE SPACE	A Character Doesn't Like Christmas	A Proposal
Has Child From Previous Marriage	Santa!	Christmas Tree in Restaurant/ Cafe	Hot Cocoa	Vehicle Breaks Down
"I Love You"	Product Placement for Advertise- ment	Leading Man Drives Pickup Truck	Must Raise Money	Amazing Baker/ Cook

Christmas Movie Bingo Card 34

Christmas Movie Bingo Card 35

Christmas Eve Deadline	Someone Wears an Apron	Montage for the Main Characters	Stuck in Small Town for Christmas	Aerial Shot of Town Decorated for Christmas
Someone says "Christmas Miracle" or "Christmas Magic"	Opening Gifts	An Old Flame Reappears	Can't Stay in Town for Long	Pre-Holiday Breakup
Character is Royalty	Red Winter Coat	FREE SPACE	Kiss Under the Mistletoe	Wearing Mittens (Not Gloves)
Wrapping Presents	Roads are Closed	Snowed In	An Injury	Doing Something for Charity
Driving in Bad Weather	Character Returns Home to Small Town	Cancelled Flight	Shirtless Man	Someone is Lying

Christmas Movie Bingo Card 36

Sledding or Ice Skating	An Old Flame Reappears	Christmas Pajamas	Live Christmas Music	A Nutcracker Decoration
Someone Gets Fired	It's Snowing!	Mis-under-standing Keeps Them Apart	Putting up Lights Outside	Snow Globe
Santa Suit	Declined Phone Call	FREE SPACE	Someone Cries	Sheriff or Doctor is a Main Character
Small Diner or Cafe	Someone is Stranded	Singing a Christmas Carol While Working	Making a Family Recipe	Hot Cocoa
Special Christmas Ornament	Town Event in Jeopardy	Someone is a Scrooge	Main Character Lost a Parent	Baking Christmas Cookies

Christmas Movie Bingo Card 37

Red Winter Coat	"I Love You"	Sledding or Ice Skating	Christmas Themed Joke	Match-maker Friend/ Family Member
Small Diner or Cafe	A Man with a Holiday Themed Name	Takes a Selfie Photo	Montage for the Main Characters	Someone is Stranded
A Christmas Play or Concert	Someone is a Scrooge	**FREE SPACE**	Wrapping Presents	Real Snow
Sitting by the Fireplace	An Apology	Childhood Home/ Lodge/ Getaway	Secondary Love Story with Secondary Characters	Lose the Contest/ Competition
A Family Heirloom	Baking Christmas Cookies	A Contest	Church Service Scene	Someone is a Work-a-holic

Christmas Movie Bingo Card 38

Went to High School Together	Jealousy	Someone Wears an Apron	Coffee Shop	Looking at Old Pictures
An Almost Kiss	City Scene During Opening Credits	Town Event in Jeopardy	Job Offer	Baking Christmas Cookies
Making a Snowman	Florida is Mentioned	**FREE SPACE**	Wearing Mittens (Not Gloves)	Santa Suit
Dream Job	Don't Like Each Other at First	Live Christmas Music	Deceased Parent	Love Triangle
Sticker Over the Laptop Logo	Christmas Tree Falls Over	Must Raise Money	Opening Gifts	Wise Words from a Parent

Christmas Movie Bingo Card 39

Ginger-bread Houses	First Kiss is the Last Scene	Running Late	An Apology	Hot Cocoa
Looking at Old Pictures	Up for Promotion	Fireplace Scene	Accidental Fall	Wearing a Santa Hat with Normal Clothes
Montage for the Main Characters	Kiss Under the Mistletoe	**FREE SPACE**	Christmas Tree in Restaurant/Cafe	An Inn
Snowball Fight	Christmas Caroling	Everyone Around the Table for Dinner	It's Snowing!	Ugly Christmas Sweater
A Proposal	Pretend to be the Girlfriend/ Boyfriend/ Fiancé	Someone is Wearing Plaid	Declined Phone Call	Sledding or Ice Skating

Christmas Movie Bingo Card 40

Main Character has an Office Job	Shopping for a Christmas Tree	Win the Contest/ Competition	A Woman with a Holiday Themed Name	Character Makes a U-Turn, Literally or Figuratively
Someone is a Work-a-holic	An Almost Kiss	Leading Man Drives Pickup Truck	Christmas Eve Deadline	Thanks-giving Dinner
Town Event in Jeopardy	Amnesia	**FREE SPACE**	Wrapping Presents	An Airport Scene
A Gazebo	Sitting by the Fireplace	A Scene When It's Not Winter	"I Love You"	Outsider Puts on Tree Topper
Bump into Each Other	Doing Something for Charity	Christmas Shopping	Went to High School Together	Amazing Baker/ Cook

Christmas Movie Bingo Card 42

Christmas Movie Bingo Card 41

Everyone Around the Table for Dinner	Holds Mug with Two Hands	Surprise Decorating for Christmas	An Apology	Remake of Classic Christmas Song Plays
A Nutcracker Decoration	Dream Job	Sleigh Ride	Must Raise Money	Looking at Old Pictures
Character is Actually the Real Santa	Hot Cocoa	**FREE SPACE**	Wise Parental Advice	City Scene During Opening Credits
Someone is a Scrooge	Decorating a Christmas Tree	Driving in Bad Weather	Small Diner or Cafe	Someone Wears an Apron
Blindfold or Covering Eyes	An Inn	Single Parent	Decorating a Christmas Tree	Live Christmas Music

Christmas Movie Bingo Card 4

Christmas Movie Bingo Card 42

Making a Family Recipe	Christmas Shopping	Gingerbread Houses	Florida is Mentioned	Reindeer
Weather Interferes with Plans	Someone is Stranded	"I Love You"	Son/Daughter Wants Their Mom/Dad to Get Married	It's Snowing!
Holds Mug with Two Hands	Jingling Bells	**FREE SPACE**	Fake Snow	Aerial Shot of Town Decorated for Christmas
A Gift of Jewelry	A Character Who Loves Christmas	Lose the Contest/ Competition	Baking Christmas Cookies	Character is Royalty
Love Triangle	A Proposal	Ugly Christmas Sweater	Wrapping Presents	Doing Something for Charity

Christmas Movie Bingo

Christmas Movie Bingo Card 43

Don't Like Each Other at First	Doing Something for Charity	It's Snowing!	Christmas Tree Falls Over	A Kiss with a Foot Pop
Opening Gifts	Hot Cocoa	A Christmas Play or Concert	Santa Suit	A Christmas Party
Special Family Tradition	Can't Stay in Town for Long	**FREE SPACE**	Someone Cries	Green Grass
Decorating a Christmas Tree	An Inn	Christmas Tree in Restaurant/ Cafe	Someone is Lying	Red Winter Coat
Amazing Baker/ Cook	Teacher	An Old Flame Reappears	"Open" Sign at a Business	Town Event in Jeopardy

Christmas Movie Bingo Card 44

Wearing a Santa Hat with Normal Clothes	Accidental Fall	Someone is Stranded	An Apology	Childhood Home/ Lodge/ Getaway
Pre-Holiday Breakup	Wrapping Presents	Tree Lighting	Has Child From Previous Marriage	Making a Family Recipe
Sledding or Ice Skating	Aerial Shot of Town Decorated for Christmas	FREE SPACE	A Proposal	Small Diner or Cafe
A Contest	Kiss Under the Mistletoe	Concerned Family Member	Singing a Christmas Carol While Working	Dancing
Wearing Mittens (Not Gloves)	Sticker Over the Laptop Logo	New York is Mentioned	Aerial Shot of a Small Town	Small Diner or Cafe

Christmas Movie Bingo Card 45

A Barn	An Apology	Wearing Mittens (Not Gloves)	Jealousy	Singing a Christmas Carol While Working
Former Girlfriend/ Boyfriend	Baking Christmas Cookies	Sledding or Ice Skating	Roads are Closed	Wears a Fancy Dress
Decorating a Christmas Tree	Match-maker Friend/ Family Member	**FREE SPACE** 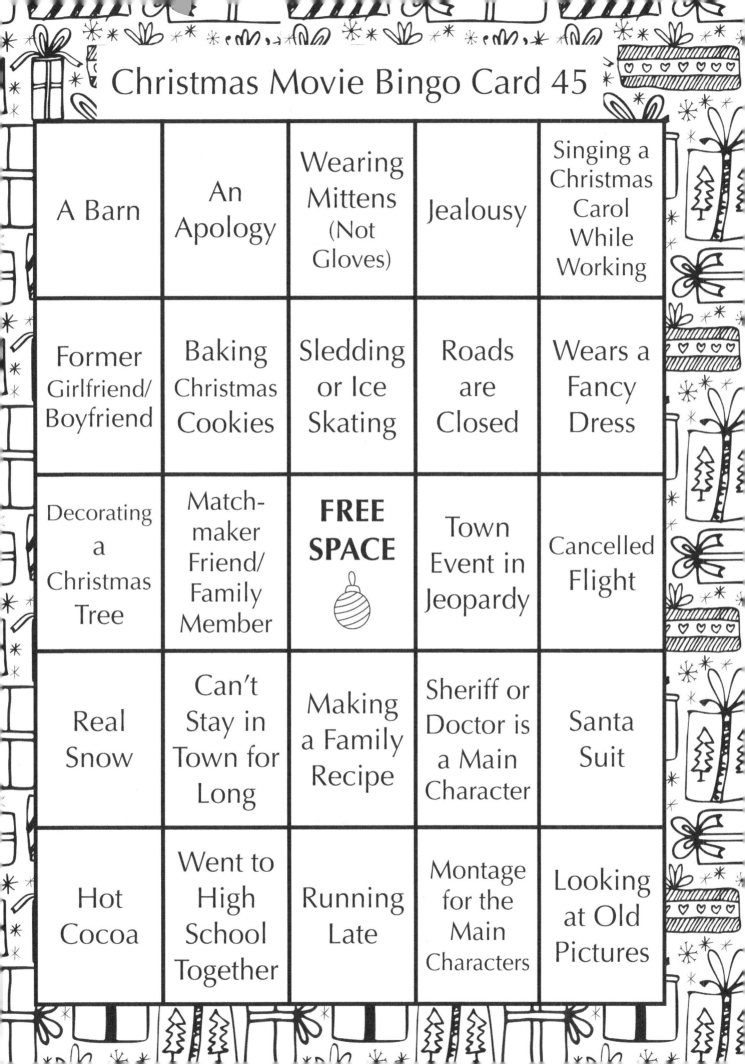	Town Event in Jeopardy	Cancelled Flight
Real Snow	Can't Stay in Town for Long	Making a Family Recipe	Sheriff or Doctor is a Main Character	Santa Suit
Hot Cocoa	Went to High School Together	Running Late	Montage for the Main Characters	Looking at Old Pictures

Christmas Movie Bingo Card 46

Inherits a Building	Someone Winks	Sleigh Ride	Santa Suit	"I Love You"
A Man with a Holiday Themed Name	A Wedding Scene	Bad Baker/ Cook	Secondary Love Story with Secondary Characters	Characters go to a Fancy Restaurant
Child Wise Beyond Their Years	Wise Parental Advice	**FREE SPACE**	Christmas Tree in Restaurant/ Cafe	Obnox-ious Girlfriend or Boyfriend
Thanks-giving Dinner	Welcome to Town Sign	Dream Job	Fireplace Scene	Movie Opens with an Office Scene
Win the Contest/ Competition	Someone Wears an Apron	A Dog	Someone is a Work-a-holic	Riding in a Taxi

Christmas Movie Bingo Card 94

Christmas Movie Bingo Card 47

Character Returns Home to Small Town	Snow Globe	Quits Their Job	Someone Cries	Dream Job
Baking Christmas Cookies	Nativity Scene	Must Raise Money	Town has a Holiday Themed Name	Christmas Tree Farm
A Character Doesn't Like Christmas	Live Christmas Music	**FREE SPACE**	Someone is a Scrooge	Stuck in Small Town for Christmas
Wise Parental Advice	Santa Gives Sage Advice	Sitting by the Fireplace	Christmas Themed Joke	Decorating a Christmas Tree
Everyone Around the Table for Dinner	Character is Actually the Real Santa	It's Snowing!	Niece or Nephew	Childhood Home/ Lodge/ Getaway

Christmas Movie Bingo Card 48

Wise Parental Advice	Looking at Old Pictures	Main Character has an Office Job	Christmas Eve Deadline	"Open" Sign at a Business
Santa Suit	A Woman with a Holiday Themed Name	Don't Like Each Other at First	Shopping for a Christmas Tree	Snowball Fight
Love Triangle	It's Snowing!	FREE SPACE	Small Town Business is in Trouble	Lose the Contest/ Competition
Holiday Party	Christmas Tree Falls Over	Someone is a Scrooge	Amazing Baker/ Cook	Declined Phone Call
Movie Opens with a Baking Scene	Character is Royalty	Road Trip	A Character Who Loves Christmas	Sitting by the Fireplace

Christmas Movie Bingo Card 49

Remake of Classic Christmas Song Plays	Working on Christmas	Up for Promotion	Santa!	Man in a Flannel Shirt
An Inn	Driving in Bad Weather	Wrapping Presents	Someone Cries	Ugly Christmas Sweater
Went to High School Together	Concerned Family Member	**FREE SPACE**	Making a Family Recipe	Don't Like Each Other at First
Shirtless Man	City Scene During Opening Credits	Christmas Shopping	An Apology	Town Event in Jeopardy
An Old Flame Reappears	Fireplace Scene	Snowed In	A Scene When It's Not Winter	An Almost Kiss

Christmas Movie Bingo Card 50

"I Love You"	Baking Christmas Cookies	Red Winter Coat	Christmas Caroling	Kiss Under the Mistletoe
Mis-under-standing Keeps Them Apart	Christmas Shopping	Someone says "Christmas Miracle" or "Christmas Magic"	Under-cover Assignment	Baking Christmas Cookies
Small Diner or Cafe	Characters Get Engaged	**FREE SPACE**	Wise Parental Advice	Doing Something for Charity
Dream Job	Montage for the Main Characters	Hot Cocoa	Bump into Each Other	Vehicle Breaks Down
Deceased Parent	Someone is Lying	Gingerbread Houses	Video Chat	Weather Interferes with Plans

See Amazon for more volumes of Christmas Movie Bingo!

Christmas Movie Bingo By Nannette Smith

Made in United States
North Haven, CT
17 December 2024